T0379159

Thinking Critically:
Addiction

Carla Mooney

ReferencePoint
Press®

San Diego, CA

© 2023 ReferencePoint Press, Inc.
Printed in the United States

For more information, contact:
ReferencePoint Press, Inc.
PO Box 27779
San Diego, CA 92198
www.ReferencePointPress.com

ALL RIGHTS RESERVED.
No part of this work covered by the copyright hereon may be reproduced or used in any form or by any means—graphic, electronic, or mechanical, including photocopying, recording, taping, web distribution, or information storage retrieval systems—without the written permission of the publisher.

LIBRARY OF CONGRESS CATALOGING-IN-PUBLICATION DATA

Names: Mooney, Carla, 1970- author.
Title: Thinking critically : addiction / Carla Mooney.
Other titles: Addiction
Description: San Diego, CA : ReferencePoint Press, Inc., [2023] | Series:
   Thinking critically | Includes bibliographical references and index.
Identifiers: LCCN 2021061324 (print) | LCCN 2021061325 (ebook) | ISBN
   9781678203122 (library binding) | ISBN 9781678203139 (ebook)
Subjects: LCSH: Drug addiction--United States--Juvenile literature. | Drug
   addiction--Treatment--United States--Juvenile literature. | Substance
   abuse--United States--Juvenile literature. | Substance
   abuse--Treatment--United States--Juvenile literature.
Classification: LCC RC564.3 .M66 2023 (print) | LCC RC564.3 (ebook) | DDC
   362.29--dc23/eng/20220114
LC record available at https://lccn.loc.gov/2021061324
LC ebook record available at https://lccn.loc.gov/2021061325

Contents

Foreword   4

Overview: What Is Addiction?   6

Chapter One: Is Addiction a Disease or a Choice?
The Debate at a Glance   13
Addiction Is a Disease   14
Addiction Is a Choice   21

Chapter Two: Should Medication-Assisted Treatment Be Used to Treat Addiction?
The Debate at a Glance   26
Medication-Assisted Treatment Should Be Used   27
Medication-Assisted Treatment Should Not Be Used   33

Chapter Three: Should the United States Decriminalize Drugs?
The Debate at a Glance   39
The United States Should Decriminalize Drugs   40
The United States Should Not Decriminalize Drugs   46

Source Notes   52
Addiction Facts   55
Related Organizations and Websites   57
For Further Research   59
Index   60
Picture Credits   64
About the Author   64

Foreword

"Literacy is the most basic currency of the knowledge economy we're living in today." Barack Obama (at the time a senator from Illinois) spoke these words during a 2005 speech before the American Library Association. One question raised by this statement is: What does it mean to be a literate person in the twenty-first century?

E.D. Hirsch Jr., author of *Cultural Literacy: What Every American Needs to Know*, answers the question this way: "To be culturally literate is to possess the basic information needed to thrive in the modern world. The breadth of the information is great, extending over the major domains of human activity from sports to science."

But literacy in the twenty-first century goes beyond the accumulation of knowledge gained through study and experience and expanded over time. Now more than ever literacy requires the ability to sift through and evaluate vast amounts of information and, as the authors of the Common Core State Standards state, to "demonstrate the cogent reasoning and use of evidence that is essential to both private deliberation and responsible citizenship in a democratic republic."

The Thinking Critically series challenges students to become discerning readers, to think independently, and to engage and develop their skills as critical thinkers. Through a narrative-driven, pro/con format, the series introduces students to the complex issues that dominate public discourse—topics such as gun control and violence, social networking, and medical marijuana. All chapters revolve around a single, pointed question such as Can Stronger Gun Control Measures Prevent Mass Shootings?, or Does Social Networking Benefit Society?, or Should Medical Marijuana Be Legalized? This inquiry-based approach introduces student researchers to core issues and concerns on a given topic. Each chapter includes one part that argues the affirmative and one part that argues the negative—all written by a single author. With the single-author format the predominant arguments for and against an issue can be synthesized into clear, accessible discussions supported by details and evidence including relevant facts, direct quotes, current examples, and statistical illustrations. All volumes include focus questions to guide students as they read each pro/con discussion, a list of key facts, and an annotated list of related organizations and websites for conducting further research.

The authors of the Common Core State Standards have set out the particular qualities that a literate person in the twenty-first century must have. These include the ability to think independently, establish a base of knowledge across a wide range of subjects, engage in open-minded but discerning reading and listening, know how to use and evaluate evidence, and appreciate and understand diverse perspectives. The new Thinking Critically series supports these goals by providing a solid introduction to the study of pro/con issues.

What Is Addiction?

When Dock Henry was fourteen years old, an injury landed him in the hospital, where doctors prescribed painkillers to help his recovery. The teen quickly became dependent on the prescription medication. When he was sixteen, Henry tried heroin for the first time. "I'm like, 'Whoa, this is way better and it lasted longer. This is what I like,'"[1] remembers thirty-seven-year-old Henry.

After two years of using heroin, Henry began mixing heroin with methamphetamine. When he did not use, he experienced withdrawal symptoms. "It was crazy. If I would stop using, I would get sick or what we call 'dope sick,'" says Henry. "I started getting really sick of flu-like symptoms, but I didn't know why. And then when I used heroin, I started feeling good. So for me in my active addiction, I went full bore. I never wanted to stop and didn't think I would stop,"[2] says Henry.

While Henry was actively in the grip of his drug addiction, he overdosed seven times. "That should have been a wake-up call, but it didn't slow me down then,"[3] he says. In 2015 Henry was arrested when a friend overdosed at his house. His two oldest children were taken from him and placed in temporary foster care. Still, Henry could not stop using drugs. When required to take drug tests through the Indiana Department of Child Services, he failed more than fifty of them.

After twenty-one years of addiction, Henry finally resolved to beat his drug dependence when he realized his son blamed himself for being in foster care. Henry entered treatment and lived at a facility that provided care for people with alcohol and drug addictions. He also attended counseling and group support meetings for people struggling with addiction. After nearly three years, Henry regained custody of his children. Today Henry works as a peer recovery coach and has been sober for more than four years.

Addiction Is a Widespread Problem

Henry's two-decade struggle with drug addiction is a story that occurs in communities across the United States, from big cities to small rural towns. Addiction is a serious problem that affects millions of people. More than 40 million Americans aged twelve and older lived with a substance use disorder in 2020, according to the Substance Abuse and Mental Health Services Administration (SAMHSA). People with a substance use disorder, which is the medical term for addiction, are unable to stop using a substance or engaging in a behavior even though they know it causes physical, mental, and emotional harm. "[The] data show the urgent need to intervene at every opportunity to reduce substance use disorder and meet people where they are,"[4] says Office of National Drug Control Policy acting director Regina LaBelle.

> "[The] data show the urgent need to intervene at every opportunity to reduce substance use disorder and meet people where they are."[4]
>
> —Regina LaBelle, acting director of the Office of National Drug Control Policy

Over time, addiction can seriously interfere with and disrupt a person's daily life. A person dealing with an addiction may go through mild and intense use, relapse, and remission cycles. Over time, however, an untreated addiction will typically worsen and may lead to long-term health complications and other life consequences.

Types of Addictions

Many addictions involve dependence on a substance such as alcohol, nicotine, or illegal drugs. Drug addiction affects a person's brain and behavior. Drug use may start when a person uses painkillers prescribed by a doctor or experiments with alcohol or recreational drugs. When using a drug regularly, the individual might need larger doses to feel the same effects. And the more the person uses, the more difficult it becomes to go without the substance. If use is interrupted or ceases, the user may develop strong cravings and withdrawal symptoms that make him or her feel sick. The most common substances abused in addictions include alcohol, nicotine, prescription painkillers, cocaine, heroin, benzodiazepines, and stimulants.

In addition to substance addiction, some people can become addicted to certain behaviors such as gambling or working. Behavioral addiction involves an intense desire to perform certain behaviors or activities even though negative consequences result. These people compulsively crave the behavior because it creates calming feelings or euphoria, and they continue to perform the behavior even if it harms their health and daily life. Some of the most common behavioral addictions include compulsions to exercise, gamble, eat, surf the internet, and shop. Gambling addiction, however, is the only behavioral addiction currently included in the *Diagnostic and Statistical Manual of Mental Disorders*, a handbook used by medical professionals to guide their diagnosis of mental health disorders. The others have not been medically certified as addictive.

While many people can engage in compulsive activities without a problem, others can become addicted. When addiction takes over, individuals seek more opportunities to engage in the behavior. The desire to feel the "high" from the behavior becomes so strong that people continue to perform the behavior even if it has negative consequences in their life. In some cases, individuals may experience withdrawal symptoms such as negative emotions when they cannot perform the behavior.

What Causes Addiction?

Most of the time, a person initially chooses to try drugs or alcohol or behaviors like gambling. For some people, repeated use over time triggers changes in the brain that lead to addiction.

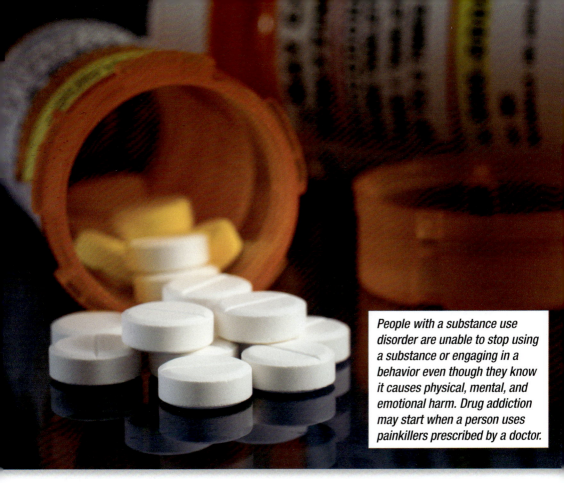

People with a substance use disorder are unable to stop using a substance or engaging in a behavior even though they know it causes physical, mental, and emotional harm. Drug addiction may start when a person uses painkillers prescribed by a doctor.

In normal circumstances, the healthy brain releases a chemical called dopamine when a person engages in rewarding behaviors such as exercise or eating good food. Dopamine reinforces these behaviors and links the pleasurable feelings produced by these behaviors with the desire to repeat them.

Drugs, alcohol, and some addictive behaviors can activate the brain's reward center and trigger a powerful release of dopamine, which trains the brain to want to repeat the actions that produced pleasurable feelings. Some addictive drugs can trigger the release of up to ten times the amount of dopamine that a natural reward does. Drugs and alcohol also activate the brain to release dopamine more quickly and reliably. The release of a large amount of dopamine at one time overwhelms the brain. The body responds by producing less dopamine or reducing the number of dopamine receptors in the brain. Thus, a person needs more of the substance to produce the same pleasurable feelings with repeated substance use, and eventually, the substance no longer produces good feelings. However, if the person stops using it, he or she experiences unpleasant withdrawal symptoms. When this occurs, the person returns to using the substance just to feel normal.

Scientists believe that behavioral addictions develop similarly. Performing a particular behavior such as gambling or exercising releases feel-good chemicals in the brain. Over time, a person relies on the behavior to avoid negative feelings.

Risk of Addiction

People of all ages, races, and social statuses develop addictions. However, certain groups of people tend to develop addiction more often than others. Research has shown that people from families with a history of addiction have a greater risk of developing an addiction themselves. According to the National Institute on Drug Abuse, as much as 50 percent of a person's risk of addiction to alcohol, nicotine, or other drugs is based on genetics and family history.

Environmental factors can also increase the risk of addiction. Lack of parental involvement can lead children and teens to experiment with alcohol and drugs. Youth who experience abuse or neglect are more likely to turn to addictive substances. Peer pressure and the availability of addictive substances can also increase substance use. Some people with mental health conditions may turn to such substances to cope with their feelings and symptoms. Over time, a person becomes more likely to develop an addiction with repeated substance use.

The type of substance and the method of use can also influence addiction risk. Some drugs, such as cocaine, heroin, and methamphetamine, are more physically addictive than marijuana or alcohol. These drugs cause more intense withdrawal symptoms, which can cause a person to use them more frequently and in greater amounts. The way a person uses drugs can also affect the risk of addiction. Drugs that are smoked or injected into the body often have a greater tendency to cause addiction than those that are swallowed. Smoking or injecting drugs sends these substances directly into the bloodstream and brain rather than filtering them through other body organs.

Treatment

Addiction is treatable. Treatment depends on the type of addiction and its severity. For most people, the traditional addiction treatment begins with a stay at an inpatient rehabilitation program, where addicts can detox from drugs or alcohol. While in rehab, patients usually participate in therapy and counseling to identify drug-use triggers and learn how to resist temptation.

Addicts can continue to participate in outpatient therapy, counseling, and group support meetings upon leaving a residential program. They may receive medications for coexisting conditions such as depression or bipolar disorder. For some people addicted to opioids, medication-assisted treatment (MAT) combines US Food and Drug Administration–approved medications with counseling and therapy to treat addiction. MAT's prescribed medications work to lessen painful withdrawal symptoms and cravings while also reducing or eliminating the opioid high.

Addiction Debate

Addictions and their treatments are topics that stir emotions and generate passionate debate. Some people believe strongly that addiction is a disease over which people have little control. Those who support this core idea frequently advocate for more compassionate treatment and care for those suffering from addiction. Yet other people strongly disagree and point to addicts' choices as being the root cause of their addiction problems. Those who view addiction from this perspective often support policies and treatments that emphasize personal responsibility in choosing to engage in addictive behavior and adhering to a recovery plan.

"The topic of addiction is often polarized. Opinions vary wildly from 'Addicts deserve what they get' to 'Addiction is a disease, and I'm a victim.'"[5]

—Jason Good, a recovered addict

Jason Good is a recovered addict who has worked in addiction and recovery for more than ten years. He believes that addiction is a complicated, nuanced issue. "The topic of addiction is often polarized," he says. "Opinions vary wildly from 'Addicts deserve what they get' to 'Addiction is a disease, and I'm a victim.' Neither viewpoint provides an entirely accurate description of the reality of addiction." No matter which viewpoint a person holds, addiction is a problem that affects a lot of people. "Addiction can strike anyone, and the road back is often a difficult one,"[5] Good says.

Chapter One

Is Addiction a Disease or a Choice?

Addiction Is a Disease

- Addiction causes changes in brain chemistry and function.
- Addiction causes physical dependency and withdrawal symptoms.
- Addiction, like other diseases such as cancer and diabetes, has a genetic risk component that makes some people more likely to develop it.

The Debate at a Glance

Addiction Is a Choice

- Addiction is a behavior that one chooses. No one chooses to develop diseases like diabetes or cancer.
- Addiction is not transmissible or contagious, autoimmune, or hereditary like many diseases. Instead, it is primarily caused by social and environmental factors.
- If addiction is a choice, recovery is possible if a person makes a choice to stop using a substance or engaging in a behavior.

Addiction Is a Disease

"One of the most common misperceptions about addiction is thinking that it is a choice, or a character flaw. It is not. It is a brain disease, a chronic, relapsing disorder characterized by compulsive drug seeking and continued use despite harmful consequences, along with changes in brain circuitry. It is considered both a complex brain disorder and a mental illness."

—Dr. Nora D. Volkow, director of the National Institute on Drug Abuse at the National Institutes of Health

Quoted in Elizabeth Yepez and Rachel Daniel, "Addiction Should Be Treated, Not Penalized: An Interview with Nora D. Volkow," *On Health* (blog), BMC, August 25, 2021. https://blogs.biomed central.com.

Consider these questions as you read:

1. Taking into account the facts and ideas presented in this discussion, how persuasive is the argument that addiction is a disease? Explain why.
2. What do you think is meant by the claim that addiction is a chronic disease? Explain whether you think this argument is accurate.
3. What effect, if any, would training more medical professionals to treat drug abuse have on addiction?

Editor's note: The discussion that follows presents common arguments made in support of this perspective, reinforced by facts, quotes, and examples taken from various sources.

A disease is an illness or abnormal condition that affects a person and prevents the body or mind from working normally. Diseases affect the structure or function of the body's organs. For example, heart disease affects the structure and function of several organs in the body's cardiovascular system: the heart, veins, and arteries. Diabetes affects the operation of the pancreas and its ability to produce necessary amounts of the hormone insulin, which regulates many processes that provide the body's cells with vital energy.

Many medical professionals agree that addiction is a chronic disease of the brain. Doctors have treated addiction since the 1800s. Organizations such as the American Medical Association and the American Society of Addiction Medicine classify addiction as a disease. In November 2016 US surgeon general Vivek Murthy released a landmark report on alcohol, drugs, and addiction that called for addiction to be treated as a disease. In the report, Murthy wrote:

"We must help everyone see that addiction is not a character flaw—it is a chronic illness that we must approach with the same skill and compassion with which we approach heart disease, diabetes, and cancer."[6]

—Dr. Vivek Murthy, US surgeon general

> We . . . need a cultural shift in how we think about addiction. For far too long, too many in our country have viewed addiction as a moral failing. This unfortunate stigma has created an added burden of shame that has made people with substance use disorders less likely to come forward and seek help. It has also made it more challenging to marshal the necessary investments in prevention and treatment. We must help everyone see that addiction is not a character flaw—it is a chronic illness that we must approach with the same skill and compassion with which we approach heart disease, diabetes, and cancer.[6]

Addiction Changes Brain Chemistry and Function

Like other diseases, addiction affects the structure and function of a body organ, the brain. Decades of research have shown that addiction causes significant changes to the brain's "wiring" and functioning. The first time people use drugs or drink alcohol, they do so voluntarily, believing that they can control their substance use. However, repeated use over time causes changes in the

Many Americans View Opioid Addiction as a Disease

More Americans view opioid addiction as a disease than as a result of a lack of willpower. In an Associated Press-NORC Center for Public Affairs Research survey, 53 percent replied that it was extremely or very likely that addiction was a medical problem that required treatment. This contrasts with 44 percent who felt that lack of willpower or discipline were to blame for addiction.

Medical Problem or Lack of Willpower?

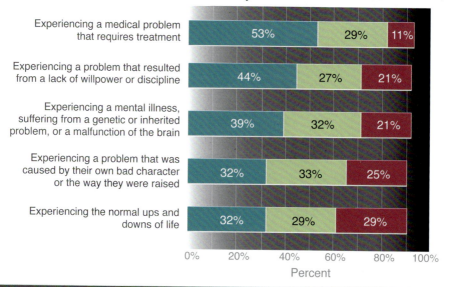

Question: *How likely is it that an addict is...*

	Extremely/very likely	Somewhat likely	Not too/not at all likely
Experiencing a medical problem that requires treatment	53%	29%	11%
Experiencing a problem that resulted from a lack of willpower or discipline	44%	27%	21%
Experiencing a mental illness, suffering from a genetic or inherited problem, or a malfunction of the brain	39%	32%	21%
Experiencing a problem that was caused by their own bad character or the way they were raised	32%	33%	25%
Experiencing the normal ups and downs of life	32%	29%	29%

Source: "Americans Recognize the Growing Problem of Opioid Addiction," Associated Press-NORC Center for Public Affairs Research, April 2018. https://apnorc.org.

brain that drive a compulsive need for the substance that becomes an addiction.

Scientists have identified several areas in the brain involved in addiction. A healthy brain is wired to reward people when they do something linked to survival, such as exercising or eating. When a person eats, the brain releases a neurotransmitter called dopamine to let the body know that it benefits by repeating that behavior. Drugs and alcohol also trigger the brain's reward system. When a person uses such a substance, the brain releases large numbers of neurotransmitters, including dopamine. When this occurs, the person experiences euphoria, a feeling of intense happiness and excitement that generates a "high." These pleasurable feelings also teach the brain that drugs are good, strongly reinforcing drug use. Dopamine is key for convincing the brain to repeat that pleasurable experience.

With repeated substance use, the brain produces less dopamine to avoid being overwhelmed by the euphoria. The number of brain structures that can receive dopamine may also decrease to counteract the large releases triggered by the substance. The dopamine has a reduced effect on the brain's reward system when this happens, and the person's experience of pleasure, reward, and motivation declines. The brain no longer functions normally. The person continues to crave the euphoric feelings, but taking the drug no longer produces the same level of satisfaction, leading to increased use and addiction. The addictive behaviors end up replacing healthy behaviors.

The changes addiction causes in the brain are long lasting and can continue well after stopping the use of drugs or alcohol. The brain has already learned that these substances produce pleasurable feelings, and it does not forget how efficient the pathway is between these triggers and their rewards. "This is why individuals risk relapse even after long periods of abstinence, and despite a relapse's potentially devastating effects,"[7] says Jillian E. Hardee, assistant professor in the Department of Psychiatry at the University of Michigan.

Addiction Can Create a Physical Dependency

Addiction's altering of the brain and the way a person experiences pleasure encourages many individuals to use drugs or alcohol regularly. This repeated use eventually leads to a physical dependence in which the body and brain rely on the substance to function. Once people become physically dependent on a substance, they can no longer choose to stop using. If they stop, the body can become violently ill with withdrawal symptoms. These physical symptoms of withdrawal mark addiction as a disease.

Withdrawal symptoms vary depending on the substance used and how long the person has been using. In general, withdrawal symptoms are often the opposite of the substance's effect on the body. For example, if a person's gastrointestinal system slows when taking opioids, withdrawal might trigger diarrhea, cramping, nausea, and vomiting. Common withdrawal symptoms include sweating, hot and cold flashes, nausea, vomiting, diarrhea, muscle aches and cramps, tremors, dehydration, increased heart rate and blood pressure, insomnia, restlessness, and seizures. Withdrawal can also trigger psychological symptoms such as agitation, irritability, anxiety, depression, and delirium.

In some cases the process of withdrawal can be as risky as using the substances. Dangerous drugs such as heroin, prescription painkillers, alcohol, and benzodiazepines produce some of the most painful withdrawal symptoms because of how they affect the body and brain. Often, patients seeking to detox from these drugs seek the help of addiction professionals because willpower alone may not be enough to resist the temptation to ease the severe withdrawal symptoms by using the substance again.

Genetic Component

Comparing addiction and heart disease illustrates how both conditions are diseases. Both impact the functioning of a body organ—the heart in heart disease and the brain in addiction. Both heart disease and addiction impact a person's quality of life and increase the risk of early death. Both are treatable to improve health and affect the organ's function. In addition, the risks of both heart disease and addiction can be minimized by following a healthy lifestyle.

Like diseases such as diabetes and cancer, addiction has a genetic component. Research has shown that addiction runs in families, and a person may be more vulnerable to addiction if a parent or sibling has an addiction. Scientists estimate that people's genes account for 40 to 60 percent of their risk of addiction. Understanding the relationship between genes and addiction is essential to learning how to treat and prevent addiction in the most vulnerable people.

Also like many other diseases, addiction is a complex disease not caused by a single gene. Instead, scientists believe that several genes influence addiction, along with environmental factors. In addition, experts believe that epigenetic factors may also be inherited; these are differences in the responses of genes to environmental factors. Dr. Kathleen Brady, vice president of research at the Medical University of South Carolina, explains:

> This isn't a gene for a specific trait necessarily. It's a gene-by-environment interaction. You can be genetically predisposed but never develop a substance use disorder because you live in a protective environment. But if you have the vulnerable gene for alcohol abuse, and you experience early life trauma of some sort, there could be epigenetic changes that lead you to have an exaggerated stress response to future stress and be more vulnerable to the development of alcohol dependence.[8]

Every person has epigenetic variations that influence whether addiction might develop. Each gene variation can increase or decrease risk. That explains why two people from the same family may have different outcomes: one becomes addicted to a substance while the other does not. "Some people will say it's a choice because, in identical twins, there are cases of one twin being addicted and one not," says Donna Newbold, a licensed professional counselor. "At this point, we know our genes interact

"Some people will say it's a choice because, in identical twins, there are cases of one twin being addicted and one not. . . . There are identical twins where one has Alzheimer's, and one doesn't. There is no debate that Alzheimer's is a disease."[9]

—Donna Newbold, a licensed professional counselor

with our environment. There are identical twins where one has Alzheimer's, and one doesn't. There is no debate that Alzheimer's is a disease."[9]

Viewing addiction as a chronic disease, as Newbold does, is essential for finding the most effective treatments. To this goal, the American College of Physicians has called for addiction to be treated like any other chronic disease. In a statement, the organization said, "Substance abuse disorders are treatable chronic medical conditions, like diabetes and hypertension, that should be addressed through expansion of evidence-based public and individual health initiatives to prevent, treat, and promote recovery."[10]

Addiction Is a Choice

"There are virtually no data in humans indicating that addiction is a disease of the brain in the way that, for instance, Huntington's or Parkinson's are diseases of the brain."

—Marc Grifell, physician, and Carl L. Hart, chair of the Department of Psychology at Columbia University

Marc Grifell and Carl L. Hart, "Is Drug Addiction a Brain Disease?," *American Scientist*, May–June 2018. www.americanscientist.org.

Consider these questions as you read:

1. Taking into account the facts and ideas presented in this discussion, how persuasive is the argument that addiction is a choice? Explain why.
2. What do you think is meant by the claim that addiction is a choice that becomes a habit? What evidence would you cite to support or refute this claim?
3. What effect, if any, do individuals' environments have on their chances of developing an addiction?

Editor's note: The discussion that follows presents common arguments made in support of this perspective, reinforced by facts, quotes, and examples taken from various sources.

Addiction is a serious issue. Across the United States, more than 40 million people aged twelve or older reported a substance use disorder involving alcohol, illicit drugs, or both, according to SAMHSA's 2020 National Survey on Drug Use and Health. Addiction can have a devastating impact on the lives of those addicted, as well as on their families and friends. Addiction may cause individuals to drop out of school, lose their job, get in trouble with the law, land in jail, and damage personal relationships. Addiction can also lead to physical and mental health problems. Yet people who are addicted to drugs, alcohol, or other destructive behaviors are struggling with a problem of their own making. Addiction is a choice.

Substance Use Is a Choice That Becomes a Habit

No one chooses to develop diseases like cancer, heart disease, or diabetes. However, addicts choose to start using drugs or alcohol or to engage in addictive behaviors. They make a conscious decision to take a drink, smoke a joint, swallow a pill, or place a gambling bet.

Over time the choice to use drugs or alcohol or to engage in certain behaviors becomes a habit. A habit is a routine behavior that occurs regularly and often without thought. A habit can be an action like drinking alcohol or a routine like getting high before a social event. Marc Lewis, a neuroscientist who believes that addiction should not be classified as a disease, says, "Rather than a disease, I would say that addiction is a habit that grows and perpetuates itself relatively quickly when we repeatedly pursue the same highly attractive goal. This results in new pathways being built in the brain, which is always the case with learning: new pathways are formed and older pathways are pruned or eradicated."[11]

> "Rather than a disease, I would say that addiction is a habit that grows and perpetuates itself relatively quickly when we repeatedly pursue the same highly attractive goal."[11]
>
> —Marc Lewis, a neuroscientist

Lewis explains that forming the habit of addiction can cause changes in the brain, just as any learning creates new neural connections. Says Lewis:

> As the addiction grows, billions of new connections form in the brain. This network of connections supports a pattern of thinking and feeling, a strengthening belief, that taking this drug, "this thing," is going to make you feel better—despite plenty of evidence to the contrary. It's motivated repetition that gives rise to what I call "deep learning." Addictive patterns grow more quickly and become more deeply entrenched than other, less rewarding habits. In general, brain changes naturally settle into brain habits—this is the case in all forms of learning.[12]

Addiction Driven by Environment and Social Choices

Sometimes people get sick because they catch a contagious disease like influenza or strep throat from another person. Infectious diseases can be transferred from one person to another via respiratory droplets, blood, or other body fluids. Other times people become sick when their body attacks and damages their tissues, like autoimmune diseases such as celiac disease or lupus. Other diseases, like cystic fibrosis or sickle-cell anemia, are caused by genetic mutations present at birth and can be passed down from parent to child.

Unlike these actual diseases, addiction is primarily caused by choices and the environment. Addiction is not contagious and

Personal Choice Plays a Role in Addiction

Many doctors, nurses, and other health care workers in the United Kingdom believe personal choice plays a role in addiction. A survey published in 2020 shows that a high percentage of respondents see personal choice as entirely, mostly, or partly a factor in cigarette, drug, and alcohol addiction.

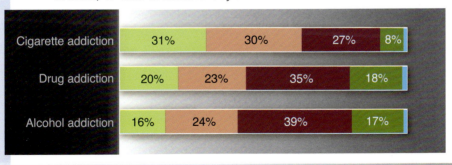

Personal Choice Is Key

When it comes to issues like addiction, do you believe the reasons why people find themselves in these situations tends to be personal choice, or due to factors beyond an individual's control?

	Entirely down to personal choice	More down to personal choice than factors beyond an individual's control	Equally personal choice and factors beyond an individual's control	More down to factors beyond an individual's control than personal choice
Cigarette addiction	31%	30%	27%	8%
Drug addiction	20%	23%	35%	18%
Alcohol addiction	16%	24%	39%	17%

- Entirely down to personal choice
- More down to personal choice than factors beyond an individual's control
- Equally personal choice and factors beyond an individual's control
- More down to factors beyond an individual's control than personal choice
- Entirely down to factors beyond an individual's control

Source: Matthew Smith, "Is Addiction a Disease or a Choice? We Ask Healthcare Workers," YouGov, January 31, 2020. https://yougov.co.uk.

cannot be transmitted from person to person. It is not the result of an autoimmune disorder or a genetic disorder passed down through families. Instead, research shows that the risk of addiction is significantly influenced by social and environmental factors. Environmental factors that impact addiction include early childhood experiences, the influence of parents and friends, cultural norms, and media representation of substance use.

A person's early life experiences often play a role in his or her choice to use drugs or alcohol. If a person experiences neglect, abuse, or addiction in the childhood home, these experiences can have a lifelong impact. Children who struggle to cope with these events are more likely to become adults who use drugs and alcohol to numb their painful emotions. "Trauma plays an incredibly huge part in addiction," says Maeve O'Neill, vice president of compliance at Vertava Health. "There are people that would say that's the root of addiction."[13] SAMHSA says that adverse childhood events increase the risk of illicit drug use and addiction up to four times. In addition, the more adverse childhood events a person experiences, the greater his or her risk of developing an addiction.

The friends and social interactions that a person chooses also significantly influence the risk of addiction. People who hang out with others who drink, smoke, and use drugs are more likely to use these substances as well. "When an individual's social interactions rely heavily on associating with individuals who display potential alcohol or drug problems, then it can be very difficult to exorcise yourself from similarly displaying such problematic behaviors," says Adi Jaffe, an expert on mental health and addiction. "The sense of belonging and feeling connected to like-minded people is a strong factor in the maintenance of addiction."[14]

Carly Benson knows firsthand how the pressure to fit in can drive a person to drink alcohol and use drugs. "After moving from Texas to Florida at age 15, I was naturally searching for new friends," she says. "Drinking seemed to be my ticket into the 'cool kids' crew. Mixed with just the right amount of curiosity and boredom, this quickly led to binge drinking and using harder drugs. By the time I was 21, I was addicted to alcohol and cocaine."[15]

Recovery Is Also a Choice

If addiction is a disease, people would be powerless to choose recovery. If it were possible to cure diseases like cancer or diabetes by choosing not to be sick, millions of people worldwide would do so. Unlike these diseases, people with an addiction can choose to become sober and stop using a substance or engaging in a behavior.

Thirty-four-year-old Dani chose to stop drinking seven years ago. "Like many who struggle with addiction, my wake-up call came in the form of a series of unfortunate events, each one a neon sign blinking, 'this is a problem,' rather than one single event,"[16] says Dani. Eventually, Dani realized she needed to change and chose to quit drinking. She says:

> "Every day it's a choice—and many days it's not an easy one. But, for me, it's always proven to be the right one."[17]
>
> —Dani, a recovering drug addict

> Every day it's a choice—and many days it's not an easy one. But, for me, it's always proven to be the right one. I never wake up with regret. I never wake up wondering where I am or who I might have been the night before. As I often say to those struggling at the beginning of sobriety: It gets easier, but it's never easy. Seven years in and there are still difficult days, but I wouldn't trade them for anything.[17]

Addiction is a serious condition that can have devastating consequences on individuals, families, and communities. However, it is important to remember that individual choice and responsibility are at the center of addiction. Without the choice to use, addiction would not occur.

Chapter Two

Should Medication-Assisted Treatment Be Used to Treat Addiction?

Medication-Assisted Treatment Should Be Used

- MAT can make stability possible in early recovery. People can give their full attention to therapy, allowing them to address the root issues that led to opiate use.
- Research shows that medication-assisted treatments work to reduce overdose deaths, keep people in treatment, and reduce relapse.
- MAT reduces the risk of infectious diseases that are spread by sharing syringes to inject drugs.

The Debate at a Glance

Medication-Assisted Treatment Should Not Be Used

- Abstinence-based treatment has a long and successful history in treating addiction.
- MAT medicines are opioids themselves. Taking drugs to quit using drugs is not a real recovery. It is simply substituting one addiction for another.
- MAT medicines can be abused. One MAT medicine, methadone, has been linked to thousands of overdose deaths annually.
- MAT medicines can have short-term and long-term side effects. Long-term use of methadone can potentially lead to changes in the brain.

Medication-Assisted Treatment Should Be Used

"Medication-assisted treatment is a game-changer. The old days of having to go through really severe DT's [detox issues] and getting really sick . . . we can shorten that. We can even prevent it with some of those drugs."

—Eric Morse, chief executive officer of Circle Health and the Centers in Cleveland

Quoted in Jonathan Walsh, "How Medication Assisted Treatment Changed One Addict's Life," News 5 Cleveland, August 31, 2021. www.news5cleveland.com.

Consider these questions as you read:

1. Taking into account the facts and ideas presented in this discussion, how persuasive is the argument that medication-assisted treatment should be used to treat addiction? Explain why.
2. What do you think is the best way to expand access to medication-assisted treatment?
3. "Do you think MAT saves lives and resources? Explain."

Editor's note: The discussion that follows presents common arguments made in support of this perspective, reinforced by facts, quotes, and examples taken from various sources.

Under traditional addiction treatment, an addict enters an inpatient rehabilitation program to detox from drugs and alcohol. While in rehab, the addict usually participates in therapy and counseling to learn how to identify drug triggers and resist temptation. However, many drug users relapse and even overdose upon leaving the residential program. Research shows that about 40 to 60 percent of people relapse within thirty days of leaving a residential treatment program, and as many as 85 percent relapse within the first year. Often they return to using drugs because they find it difficult to resist cravings and want to escape painful experiences.

MAT Allows Addicts to Focus on Recovery

Medication-assisted treatment allows people to focus on addiction recovery. MAT helps stabilize addicts early in their recovery journey. Without worrying about withdrawal symptoms and drug cravings, users can focus more fully on addiction counseling and therapy and address the root issues that led to their drug use. This gives patients the time to improve their coping skills and reduce the chances they will relapse into their addiction.

To help people break the cycle of addiction, MAT uses traditional addiction counseling and therapy, but it also incorporates US Food and Drug Administration (FDA)–approved medications

Medication-Assisted Treatment Works

The majority of medical practitioners (65 percent) rate medication-assisted treatment as the most effective way to help people with opioid addiction stop using drugs. The findings, from a 2017 survey conducted by the Economist Intelligence Unit, show that other forms of treatment are viewed as useful but not as effective.

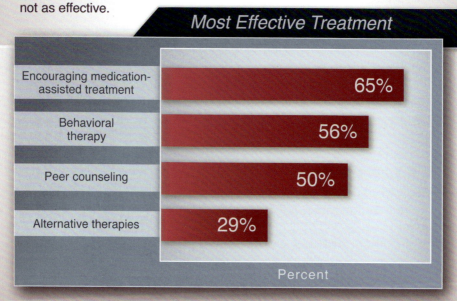

Most Effective Treatment

Treatment	Percent
Encouraging medication-assisted treatment	65%
Behavioral therapy	56%
Peer counseling	50%
Alternative therapies	29%

Percent

Source: "Briefing Paper: In-Depth Perspectives on Combating the Opioid Epidemic," The Economist Intelligence Unit, 2017. http://tacklingopioids.eiu.com.

to treat addiction. MAT medications are prescribed by a doctor and used to prevent unpleasant withdrawal symptoms, block drug cravings, and reduce or eliminate the drug's high. The FDA has approved three MAT medications to treat opioid addiction: buprenorphine, methadone, and naltrexone. Naltrexone as well as acamprosate and disulfiram are commonly used to also treat people with alcohol use disorder. While these medications do not cure the addiction, they are an effective tool for recovery as part of a MAT program.

Sarah Gad credits MAT with helping her overcome her opioid addiction. While a medical student in 2012, Gad was in a serious car accident, and doctors prescribed painkillers for her injuries. Within months Gad was addicted. Gad's life deteriorated for the next two years as her addiction grew. She says:

> Between 2013 and 2015, my life was a revolving door, in and out of jail and rehab centers. I would get arrested for a nonviolent drug offense, spend a few days in jail, get sent to rehab, then try to stay clean and get my life back on track. When I was inevitably rejected from every job I applied to—from retail to waitressing—I would start to feel hopeless, relapse, and get sent back to jail.[18]

After a jail stint in 2015, Gad overdosed on oxycodone. "Though it nearly killed me, my overdose ultimately saved me,"[19] says Gad. While she was in the hospital, doctors told her about MAT for treating opioid addiction. At first Gad was skeptical. Yet within minutes of her first dose of MAT medication, her withdrawal symptoms eased. "By the time I was released from the hospital three days later, so had my cravings." she says. "I was discharged with enough medication to last me until I could establish care with an outpatient addiction medicine specialist, which I did later that week."[20] Gad has been sober ever since.

MAT Saves Lives and Money

Numerous studies suggest that MAT can save lives and money. In one 2018 National Institutes of Health–funded study, researchers found that treatment of opioid addiction with either methadone or buprenorphine after a nonfatal opioid overdose significantly reduced opioid-related death. The researchers analyzed data from more than 17,500 people who survived an opioid overdose. For those who received methadone, overdose deaths decreased by 59 percent over the following year compared to those not receiving MAT. For participants who received buprenorphine, overdose deaths fell 38 percent compared to those who did not receive MAT. The study confirmed previous research that suggests MAT can effectively treat opioid addiction and prevent future overdose deaths. Dr. Nora D. Volkow, director of the National Institute on Drug Abuse, says:

"Decades of research show overwhelming evidence that medication for opioid use disorder, when provided promptly, can save lives."[22]

—Paul Samuels, director and president of the Legal Action Center

A great part of the tragedy of this opioid crisis is that, unlike in previous such crises America has seen, we now possess effective treatment strategies that could address it and save many lives, yet tens of thousands of people die each year because they have not received these treatments. Ending the crisis will require changing policies to make these medications more accessible and educating primary care and emergency providers, among others, that opioid addiction is a medical illness that must be treated aggressively with the effective tools that are available.[21]

Another study by researchers from several universities and state agencies published in 2020 confirmed MAT's effectiveness at preventing fatal overdose when used to treat opioid addiction.

In the study, researchers reported that people in opioid addiction treatment who received methadone or buprenorphine were 80 percent less likely to die from an opioid overdose compared to people in treatment who did not receive the medications. "Decades of research show overwhelming evidence that medication for opioid use disorder, when provided promptly, can save lives,"[22] says Paul Samuels, director and president of the Legal Action Center, a nonprofit that, in part, advocates for people with a history of addiction.

Megan Thomas believes that MAT saved her life. After her son's father was prescribed opioid painkillers, she started taking them too. "We were each probably doing 30 Percocets a day,"[23] she says. When she could not get the pills, Thomas began to snort heroin. Eventually, she began injecting heroin. In the grip of addiction, Thomas's life deteriorated. She was arrested several times. She tried addiction treatment, but nothing seemed to help her stay clean. Then after one arrest, the court ordered her to go through MAT. Thomas admits to being skeptical that the MAT medication would help her finally get clean. "But I think if you really want to be sober, it's a really amazing thing to do. Because this is the best I've ever done," says Thomas. Today she can work, take her son to child care, and complete normal daily activities without getting high. Thomas believes that MAT has transformed her life. "If it weren't for that . . . I either wouldn't be here, or I'd be in prison,"[24] she says.

> "I think if you really want to be sober, [MAT is] a really amazing thing to do. Because this is the best I've ever done."[24]
>
> —Megan Thomas, a recovering addict

Not only does MAT saves lives, it also saves money by reducing health care and criminal justice costs associated with addiction. A 2021 study published in the *Journal of the American Medical Association* analyzed one hundred thousand patients over five years. Researchers found that all forms of MAT reduced lifetime health care and criminal justice costs by $25,000 to $105,000 per person compared to no treatment.

Reducing Infectious Disease

MAT improves community health by reducing the spread of infectious diseases. Research shows that addiction and drug use increase the risk of infectious diseases in several ways. First, chronic drug and alcohol use weaken the body's immune system, increasing a person's vulnerability to various diseases. For example, chronic alcoholics have higher rates of pneumonia than people who do not drink alcohol. Regular use of opioids such as morphine, heroin, and prescription opioids weakens the immune system's ability to battle viral and bacterial diseases. For example, morphine suppresses the activity of some white blood cells, which are essential to fighting infection. As a result, people who chronically abuse morphine and other opioid drugs are more vulnerable to numerous infectious diseases than people who do not use these drugs.

In addition, the way certain drugs are used can increase the spread of infectious diseases. Drugs like heroin, cocaine, and methamphetamine can be injected directly into the bloodstream or under the skin. When drug users share nonsterile, contaminated needles and other drug-injection equipment, infectious disease is more likely to spread. Diseases such as viral hepatitis, human immunodeficiency virus (HIV), bacterial infections, and fungal infections spread among at-risk drug users via dirty needles and unsanitary conditions. According to the Centers for Disease Control and Prevention, one in ten HIV infections occurs in a person who injects drugs. According to the World Health Organization, people who inject drugs also account for an estimated 23 to 39 percent of new hepatitis C infections. Because MAT can help at-risk addicts stay clean and avoid using drugs and dirty needles, it also reduces various infectious diseases within a community.

Recovery from addiction is a complicated process. For many people, medication-assisted treatment has proved invaluable in helping them finally break the cycle of addiction and stay clean.

Medication-Assisted Treatment Should Not Be Used

"While MAT may reduce *frequency* of opioid abuse, the research shows the majority of patients still continue opioid abuse and engage in polysubstance abuse."

—Katherine Drabiak, a University of South Florida College of Public Health assistant professor specializing in health law and medical ethics

Quoted in USF Health, "Dr. Katherine Drabiak examines the use of medication assisted treatment in fight against opioid addiction," September 26, 2019. https://hscweb3.hsc.usf.edu.

Consider these questions as you read:

1. Taking into account the facts and ideas presented in this discussion, how persuasive are the arguments that medication-assisted treatment should not be used to treat addiction? Which arguments are strongest and why?
2. What are the long-term benefits of abstinence-based recovery that MAT may not provide? Is this argument convincing? Why or why not?
3. Do you think it is ever justified to use medication to combat addiction? Why or why not?

Editor's note: The discussion that follows presents common arguments made in support of this perspective, reinforced by facts, quotes, and examples taken from various sources.

Recovering from addiction is often a long and challenging process, and it takes a toll on a person physically, emotionally, and mentally. Abstinence-based recovery has a long and successful history in treating addiction. This type of recovery plan treats a person struggling with addiction without any drugs, alcohol, or other medications that may be used to ease the effects of drug withdrawal. Instead, the person overcomes addiction by entirely avoiding all addictive substances.

Alcoholics Anonymous was the first program to focus on treating addiction. Its twelve-step program emphasizes that complete abstinence from alcohol and all mind-altering substances is essential for recovery. "Successful abstinence-based approaches typically integrate community connections—12-step meetings, alumni programs, and a recovery network—as an important factor in long-term, sustainable recovery,"[25] says Dan Labuda, a counselor and program director at Northpoint Washington in Edmonds, Washington.

Over many years, this drug-free addiction treatment has proved successful for hundreds of thousands of people looking to regain their lives from addiction. Because of its record, abstinence-based treatment is the most common form of addiction treatment in the United States.

MAT Medications Are Opioids

The only way to prevent substance abuse and break the cycle of addiction is to completely avoid the substances or behaviors that trigger addiction. Under MAT, addicts may take medications for months, years, or even a lifetime as part of their treatment plan. Therefore, it is concerning that two of the three approved MAT medications for treating opioid addiction—methadone and buprenorphine—are opioids themselves. Taking one opioid drug to stop using a different opioid drug violates the core principles of abstinence-based treatment and recovery. Former US health and human services secretary Tom Price questions the use of MAT medications and says, "If we're just substituting one opioid for another, we're not moving the dial much."[26]

> "If we're just substituting one opioid for another, we're not moving the dial much."[26]
>
> —Tom Price, former US health and human services secretary

Heather Ramsey also has her doubts about MAT medications and whether they can genuinely treat people with addiction. Ramsey, who was thirty years old in 2018, has been addicted to prescription painkillers and the antianxiety medication Xanax since her teens. She sought help for her addiction because she said her body could no longer take it. When her doctor suggested MAT, Ramsey was skeptical. Although she was taking the medication, she felt guilty, as if she was not truly addressing her addiction. "I feel like I'm kind of, in a sense, cheating the program," she says, "because I'm still depending on a substance to make me feel normal, and that's not why I came here."[27]

> "I feel like I'm kind of, in a sense, cheating the program. Because I'm still depending on a substance to make me feel normal, and that's not why I came here."[27]
>
> —Heather Ramsey, an addict who has tried MAT

Sam MacMaster, the cofounder and chief clinical officer of the residential treatment program JourneyPure, worries that too many people think they can pop a pill to cure their addiction. While he admits that MAT medications can lessen withdrawal symptoms and drug cravings that drive addiction, he is concerned that people will ignore the long-proven therapies and counseling that teach them how to live a healthy life without drugs or alcohol. "My fear is we are heading in the direction where it's enough; that there's a wholly pharmaceutical solution to addiction,"[28] he says.

A woman named Kathy learned the hard way that MAT substitutes one addiction for another. Several years ago, Kathy was addicted to prescription painkillers. When she decided to get help, a friend told her about a clinic that offered methadone therapy. Although she did not know a lot about the medication, Kathy had heard it could prevent withdrawal symptoms. Wanting to avoid the nausea, sweating, aches, and diarrhea of withdrawal, Kathy decided to give methadone a try. Five years later, she takes a bus every day to the clinic, where she lines up for a daily dose of methadone. If she does not get the medication, she gets sick. Instead of freeing herself from addiction, Kathy is now tied to a different drug. She wonders whether she is better off than she was five years earlier.

MAT Medications Are Not Risk-Free

Like other opioid drugs, MAT medications can be abused. One MAT medication, methadone, is a federally designated Schedule II controlled substance, which means that while it has a legally approved use, the drug's users also have a high chance of becoming dependent on it. Other Schedule II drugs include morphine and hydrocodone.

When used as directed, methadone does not create the typical euphoria of other opioid drugs. However, when taken in high doses, methadone can cause a high and has the potential to become addictive. Even when taken as prescribed, methadone can lead to addiction. People who use methadone to treat opioid addiction are particularly vulnerable to becoming dependent because they already have a history of opioid dependency.

For some people, methadone addiction can lead to overdose. In 2019 about three thousand opioid overdose deaths were linked to methadone. Methadone overdose occurs because the drug stays in the body for a long time. Several hours after a person takes methadone and its effects have faded, the medication is still in his or her body. If the person takes another dose because the effects of the first one have worn off, the drug accumulates in the body and can lead to overdose.

Another MAT medication, buprenorphine, also has a high risk of abuse. In a survey published in 2021, researchers from the National Institute on Drug Abuse found that 25 percent of US adults who reported buprenorphine use in 2019 admitted to misusing the drug in the prior twelve months. Misuse is defined as taking the medication in larger or more frequent doses, taking it for a longer duration than prescribed by a doctor, or taking someone else's prescription.

Unwanted Side Effects

MAT medications can have unwanted short-term and long-term side effects. Methadone and buprenorphine are opioids, and they

Side Effects Are a Problem in Medication-Assisted Treatment

The risk of side effects from methadone, an opioid commonly used in medication-assisted treatment (MAT), lessens the benefits of MAT. Side effects are not uncommon—and some (such as difficulty breathing and hallucinations) can be quite serious.

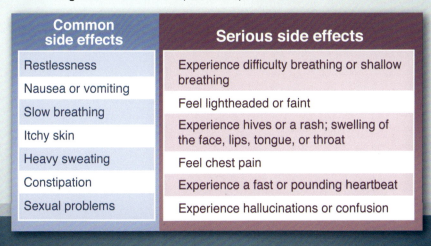

Common side effects	Serious side effects
Restlessness	Experience difficulty breathing or shallow breathing
Nausea or vomiting	
Slow breathing	Feel lightheaded or faint
Itchy skin	Experience hives or a rash; swelling of the face, lips, tongue, or throat
Heavy sweating	Feel chest pain
Constipation	Experience a fast or pounding heartbeat
Sexual problems	Experience hallucinations or confusion

Source: "Methadone," SAMHSA.gov. November 4, 2021. www.samhsa.gov.

have similar side effects. These medications may cause constipation and other gastrointestinal problems, drowsiness, dizziness, dry mouth, and sexual dysfunction. Some people experience more severe side effects from methadone, including irregular heartbeat, tremors, unstable gait, fainting, respiratory problems, seizures, and severe allergic reactions. In addition to physical side effects, methadone and other MAT medications can cause psychological side effects such as hallucinations, insomnia, depression, anxiety, and paranoia.

Over the long term, methadone can cause a physical dependency in users. If users stop taking methadone, they will experience unpleasant withdrawal symptoms associated with opioid withdrawal. Also, studies have shown that long-term use of methadone can damage a person's nerves, liver, and brain. In one study, researchers found that the brains of people who used heroin and methadone were up to three times more likely to have brain damage than people who did not use drugs. The damaged brain cells were concentrated in the parts of the brain that involve learning, memory, and emotional well-being. The damage was similar to the damage seen in the brains of early-stage Alzheimer's patients.

Medication-assisted treatment carries many risks. The medications used can cause additional addiction problems and in some cases can lead to overdose. Users often experience several unpleasant side effects, which can become long-term problems. With all of these issues, abstinence-based recovery remains the gold standard for addiction treatment.

Chapter Three

Should the United States Decriminalize Drugs?

The United States Should Decriminalize Drugs

- Decriminalization benefits public health and safety by reducing addiction, overdose, and related health and safety issues. Individuals with substance abuse problems are much more likely to find recovery in rehab than in jail.
- Drug possession arrests destroy lives. Discriminatory enforcement of these laws has produced racial and ethnic disparities at all levels of the criminal justice system.
- Other countries have successfully decriminalized drugs and not suffered detrimental consequences.

The Debate at a Glance

The United States Should Not Decriminalize Drugs

- The threat of jail deters people from using illegal drugs. Decriminalization will make people more likely to experiment with illegal drugs and eventually become addicted.
- Decriminalization would lead to an increase in crimes, including violent crime.
- The legal process provides an important path to addiction treatment and incentive for addicts to participate in court-ordered rehabilitation.

The United States Should Decriminalize Drugs

"Substance abuse has been designated by the American Medical Association as a medical diagnosis, not a moral failure, for 40 years. Yet we continue to deal with it as a criminal offense, declaring a war on drugs, with punishment rather than effective evidence-based medical treatment."

—Dr. John French, a physical medicine and rehabilitation doctor

John French, "Oregon Opportunity: Remove Criminal Penalties for Low-Level Possession of Controlled Substances," *Salem (OR) Statesman Journal*, September 18, 2020. www.statesman journal.com.

Consider these questions as you read:

1. Taking into account the facts and ideas presented in this discussion, how persuasive is the argument that the United States should decriminalize drugs? Explain why.
2. Do you think the decriminalization of drugs is equivalent to their legalization? What evidence leads you to your conclusion?
3. What effect, if any, would decriminalizing drugs have on the number of people seeking treatment for addiction?

Editor's note: The discussion that follows presents common arguments made in support of this perspective, reinforced by facts, quotes, and examples taken from various sources.

Addiction is a chronic disease. People who suffer from addiction should be given treatment, counseling, and support, not prosecuted and thrown in jail. To do this, the United States should decriminalize drugs. Decriminalizing drugs does not mean making all drug use legal. Distribution and sale of controlled substances would remain a criminal offense. However, the possession and use of drugs would be considered a public health problem and not a criminal offense. Instead of police and prisons, substance abuse and addiction cases would be treated by the professionals best equipped to handle them—addiction counselors, social workers, and psychologists.

Decriminalization Benefits Public Health and Safety

Decriminalization benefits public health and safety by reducing addiction, overdose, and related health and safety concerns. Individuals with addiction problems are more likely to find effective help in treatment programs than in prison, where drug rehabilitation programs, if they exist, are often inadequate. "When we stigmatize the problem by criminalizing a medical condition, we make it harder to seek help and receive treatment. Our current system is often inhumane and ineffective,"[29] says John French, a physical medicine and rehabilitation doctor. People completing treatment can become productive members of society much more easily than convicted felons.

Julie Eldred is one example of how treatment, not jail, can reduce addiction and improve public health. Eldred began misusing drugs at age fifteen. Over the next decade, she developed a full-blown addiction to opioids, snorting heroin or fentanyl. After she was arrested for stealing jewelry to pay for drugs in 2016, the courts granted Eldred probation and ordered her to begin addiction treatment. She complied with the judge's conditions and enrolled in an intensive, full-day outpatient addiction treatment program. However, when she relapsed days into her program, the court sent her back to prison. Behind bars, Eldred did not receive any drug counseling or medication to help her battle her addiction, and drugs were often available to the inmates.

"When we stigmatize the problem by criminalizing a medical condition, we make it harder to seek help and receive treatment. Our current system is often inhumane and ineffective."[29]

—John French, a physical medicine and rehabilitation doctor

Eldred's lawyer, Lisa Newman-Polk, convinced a judge that Eldred would be better served in treatment than in jail. The judge agreed to release Eldred if she attended residential addiction treatment. Upon her release from prison, Eldred entered a residential program, where she stayed for the next eight months. Nearly a year later, she got the help she needed to get clean and stay off drugs. Her lawyer insists that treatment, not jail, is what allowed Eldred to get better. "Dehumanizing Julie with jail didn't get her better," says Newman-Polk. "She's in recovery because of sustained treatment with medication and family support, which is exactly what the court interrupted by jailing her."[30]

In the United States, addiction and related overdoses have become a public health crisis. In fact, in the twelve months ending in April 2021, drug overdose deaths soared to over one hundred thousand, a record number, according to the Centers for Disease Control and Prevention. Robert A. Lowe and Ray G. Stangeland are two emergency room doctors in Oregon who have seen addiction's impact on people, families, and communities. "We have seen how addiction wreaks havoc on the sufferers' physical health and mental and emotional well-being, the toll addiction takes on families and communities and the difficulties for people with addictions to find a way out," Lowe and Stangeland wrote in a September 2020 editorial. The doctors firmly believe that addiction cannot be adequately treated from jail, and they support Oregon's legislation to decriminalize drugs that took effect in February 2021. "Incarceration for addiction makes matters much worse for everyone and exacerbates the untreated health complications of those with addiction," the doctors wrote. "Without access to drug treatment and recovery services, the cycle of drug use/jail time/and back on the street continues, with no support to help people find a way out."[31]

> "Incarceration for addiction makes matters much worse for everyone and exacerbates the untreated health complications of those with addiction."[31]
>
> —Robert A. Lowe and Ray G. Stangeland, emergency room doctors

Drug Possession Arrests Hurt Families and Produce Racial and Ethnic Disparities

Criminalizing drug use and possession hurts individuals, families, and communities. According to a 2020 report from the Prison Policy Initiative, police make over 1 million drug possession arrests each year. That number is six times the number of arrests for drug sales. Thousands of those arrested are held in jail before their trial because they cannot afford bail. In addition, nonviolent drug offenses lead to the incarceration of nearly half a million people on any given day. Many of these people are serving sentences of a year or longer for possession charges. With every additional arrest, people struggling with addiction are at risk for increased sentence time.

Being arrested for drugs gives those charged criminal records, making it more difficult for them to get and hold a job, and increases their likelihood of receiving a harsher sentence for any future criminal offenses. People with drug offenses have been banned from receiving federal public assistance and housing benefits, student aid, and veterans' benefits. These consequences make it more difficult for people with drug convictions to live drug-free and become productive members of society.

Also, discrimination in the enforcement of drug possession laws has led to racial and ethnic disparities across the criminal justice system. According to a 2018 report by the Drug Policy Alliance, Black people make up 13 percent of the US population, and studies show they use drugs at similar rates as other races. However, Black people make up 29 percent of those arrested for drug law violations. Nearly 40 percent of those incarcerated in state prisons for drug possession are Black. For Latinos, the pattern of discrimination is similar. According to the same Drug Policy Alliance report, Latinos make up 18 percent of the US population but are 38 percent of the people incarcerated in federal prisons for drug offenses. "For decades, the War on Drugs has been a tool to target Black and Brown Americans and change life trajectories in those communities for millions of people,"[32] says John Hudak, deputy director of the Center for Effective Public

Decriminalizing Drugs Could Reduce Arrests for Nonviolent Drug Crimes

Drug possession, which is often a nonviolent crime, accounts for more than 1 million arrests each year in the United States. These statistics, from a 2020 report from the Prison Policy Initiative, highlight how much time and resources could be diverted to improve addiction treatment programs if drug decriminalization occurred.

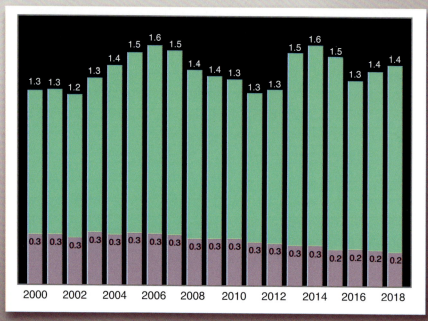

Annual Drug Possession Arrests

Note: Arrests in Millions

Source: Wendy Sawyer and Peter Wagner, "Mass Incarceration: The Whole Pie 2020," Prison Policy Initiative, March 24, 2020. www.prisonpolicy.org.

Management and a senior fellow in governance studies at the Brookings Institution.

In addition, the criminalization of drug use and possession has led to mass detentions and deportations in the United States. Noncitizens who have been in the United States for many years, working and raising families, can be automatically detained and deported if arrested for drug possession. Often these people are deported without the possibility of returning to the country.

Success in Other Countries

To see how decriminalizing drug offenses can be successfully implemented, one only needs to look at the examples already set by other countries. One of the most notable examples is Portugal, which became the first country to decriminalize low-level drug possession offenses and use of all illegal drugs in 2001. Under Portuguese law, drug dealing is still a criminal offense punishable by prison. However, anyone caught with less than a ten-day supply of any drug is sent to see a local commission consisting of a social worker, doctor, and lawyer. At the commission, the person learns about addiction treatment and available medical services.

In Portugal today, there are no arrests or incarcerations for drug possession, and more people with addictions are receiving proper treatment. Addiction, drug overdoses, and diseases like HIV that are often spread among drug users have all significantly decreased. "The Portuguese experience demonstrates that ending drug criminalization—alongside a serious investment in treatment and harm reduction services—can significantly improve public safety and health,"[33] says Jag Davies, director of communications strategy at the Drug Policy Alliance.

In 2017 Portuguese photographer Gonçalo Fonseca spent three months traveling and working with one of Lisbon's drug outreach teams. He believes that the rest of the world can learn from how Portugal handles drug use. "Drug addiction is something that will always exist," Fonseca says. However, decriminalizing drug use has eliminated the threat of criminal penalties and the stigma that goes with them, making it easier for people struggling with addiction to seek treatment. "What America and other countries can learn from Portugal is to treat people with more dignity,"[34] he says.

Drug decriminalization eliminates the criminal penalties for drug use and possession. It does not mean allowing unrestricted drug access and use across the country. Users would still be punished for using drugs in public and dealing drugs to others. However, the problem of addiction would be better treated as a medical issue than a legal one.

The United States Should Not Decriminalize Drugs

"As an African American man, I don't want more policing any time, any way. Yet I know I have colleagues who would not be alive without going to jail. There is for some people no rock bottom. For some people, they are going to die unless that intervention is there."

—Reginald Richardson Sr., executive director of Oregon's Alcohol and Drug Policy Commission

Quoted in Dirk Vanderhart, "Oregon's Pioneering Drug Law Raises More Questions than Answers in Early Months," OPB, October 27, 2021. www.opb.org.

Consider these questions as you read:

1. Taking into account the facts and ideas presented in this discussion, how persuasive is the argument that the United States should not decriminalize drugs? Explain why.
2. Do you think decriminalization of drugs is ever justified as a means to reduce addiction? Why or why not?
3. What effect, if any, would strengthening enforcement of existing criminal penalties have on individuals, families, and communities?

Editor's note: The discussion that follows presents common arguments made in support of this perspective, reinforced by facts, quotes, and examples taken from various sources.

Addiction is a problem, but decriminalizing drugs is not the solution. The threat of criminal charges is a powerful tool to deter people from using illegal drugs. When people are arrested for drug offenses, they risk going to prison. Even those who avoid jail time deal with the stigma of arrest and its negative effect on their ability to get a job, go to school, and find housing. Decriminalization of drugs removes this deterrent, and people will be more likely to experiment with illegal drugs, which will lead to more people eventually becoming addicted.

Oregon's experience highlights the flaws in decriminalizing drug use and possession. In February 2021 Oregon implemented a new approach to drug use when the state's voters decided that low-level drug possession should not be treated as a crime. Under the new law, people in Oregon who were caught using drugs or possessing illegal substances would no longer face the threat of arrest and possible jail time. Instead, the state would treat addiction and drug use as a health problem. Rather than arresting users, law enforcement hands out violations to them, similar to traffic tickets and carrying a maximum $100 fine. The ticket and fine can be dismissed if users call a hotline that conducts a brief health screening and helps them find treatment in their area. Supporters of the approach claim that it directs drug users to improved treatment options without severe penalties or a criminal record.

However, within a year of Oregon's changes, problems became apparent. Across the state, law enforcement agencies have been reluctant to hand out violations to users. And when the police do hand out the new violation tickets, drug users frequently ignore them. As of October 1, 2021, more than three-fifths of defendants were no-shows for their scheduled court dates. Even more concerning, the hotline designed to direct drug users to addiction treatment programs is quiet. As of October 2021, the line was getting an average of fewer than two calls a week from people who have received violation tickets. Less than 1 percent of people who received violations called the hotline to have their case dismissed. "I think it begs the question: Are the citizens getting what they were promised in terms of what this measure would do?" says Reginald Richardson Sr., executive director of Oregon's Alcohol and Drug Policy Commission. "I think the answer is a resounding, 'Not yet.'"[35]

Even some former addicts acknowledge that the threat of criminal charges is necessary to help some addicts choose to get clean. "I thought this ticket model was just a horrible idea and a huge waste of time and money," says recovering methamphetamine and heroin addict Tony Vezina, executive director of 4th Dimension Recovery Center and chair of the state's Alcohol and Drug Policy Commission. "If you talk to people in recovery, not all of them but a lot of people will say, 'The criminal justice system saved my life.'"[36]

Increase in Crime

Decriminalizing drug offenses may reduce the number of people arrested for drug use and possession. Still, it would likely lead to an increase in other crimes, including violent crimes. Crimes such as vehicle theft, burglary, identity theft, shoplifting, and embezzlement are often committed to pay for a substance abuse problem. "Stealing money and property to fund the addiction is a motivation listed in criminal complaints all too often; those same complaints often include child neglect and disorderly conduct. If possession alone is ignored or just a slap on the wrist, there is nothing to stop more serious crimes from happening in the future,"[37] writes John Sloca, editor for the *Kenosha News* in Wisconsin.

> "If possession alone is ignored or just a slap on the wrist, there is nothing to stop more serious crimes from happening in the future."[37]
>
> —John Sloca, editor for the *Kenosha News*

Drugs and alcohol reduce self-control, which in turn can lead to violent behaviors. Over the years, numerous studies have demonstrated a correlation between violent behaviors and substance abuse. For example, one study published in the *Journal of Substance Abuse Treatment* found that more than 75 percent of people who started drug addiction treatment reported having performed violent acts such as mugging, physical assault, and attacking another person with a weapon.

Addiction and substance abuse are also strongly linked to domestic violence. According to the American Society of Addiction

Drug Arrests Are the Only Route to the Benefits of Drug Courts

Drug courts help addicts rebuild their lives but only after they have been arrested. For this reason, drug offenses should not be decriminalized. Drug courts offer an alternative to prison as long as the offender remains in a court-sanctioned and court-supervised drug treatment program. This unique program has been successful. Statistics from Pennsylvania show a high success rate for drug courts in that state in 2020, with a significant percentage of graduates working in a job at the end of the program.

Drug Court Success Rate

- Successful
- Unsuccessful
- Unsure

64% 27% 9%

Source: "Adult Drug Courts Data," Unified Judicial System of Pennsylvania, 2020. www.pacourts.us.

Medicine, substance abuse is involved in about 40 to 60 percent of all domestic violence incidents.

In Seattle, Washington, an increase in crime and drugs threatens the city's businesses and tourism industry. Seattle crime data show a 43 percent increase in in-person crimes such as aggravated assault, robbery, rape, and homicide from 2016 to 2018. Many people who work and live in downtown Seattle complain that drug addiction is constantly on display. Many of the city's residents blame rising crime rates directly on lax enforcement of drug use and possession laws. In a 2019 editorial, the *Seattle Times* editorial board wrote:

> Seattle is in a crisis of its own making, with soaring crime in parts of the city enabled by lax enforcement and prosecution. This is making Seattle unsafe in some neighborhoods. Drug addiction is a root cause, but political dysfunction is

exacerbating the problem by allowing prolific offenders to repeatedly steal, threaten and attack people with little consequence. This is causing substantial harm, not only to individuals but the city's appeal as a place to raise families, create jobs and provide opportunity.[38]

An Important Path to Treatment

The criminal justice system provides an important path to addiction treatment for many people. While some people seek treatment for addiction on their own, others need the push from the criminal justice system and the incentive to participate in court-ordered rehabilitation. "Most people struggling with addiction can't stop using drugs on their own. If they could, they wouldn't be addicted. However, many people in long-term recovery credit the motivation of court diversion programs with 'saving my life' or 'rescuing me from myself,'"[39] write Heather Jefferis, executive director of the Oregon Council for Behavioral Health, and Se-ah-dom Edmo, cochair of the Oregon Recovers advocacy group for people in recovery from addiction.

In a court diversion program, a judge sentences drug offenders to mandatory addiction treatment instead of jail time. Defendants must complete the court-ordered program, and if they do not, they can be sent to jail. Court-ordered rehabilitation aims to help those addicted to drugs or alcohol and prevent future crimes. If drug crimes are decriminalized, the courts will have no authority to push people who need addiction treatment to get it.

MacKenzie Schreiber credits court-ordered rehabilitation with helping her get sober for the first time in years. Schreiber began using drugs as a teenager and eventually became addicted to heroin and methamphetamine. She drifted in and out of treatment centers, jail, and living on the streets for fifteen years. After giving birth to her son, Schreiber committed herself to kicking her drug addiction. She spent a few months in jail after another drug charge before being transferred to a drug court program, where she committed to addiction therapy and meetings. In May 2021 Schreiber graduated from the drug court program. "I wouldn't be standing here today if it wasn't for drug court," she says. "They are some of the biggest supporters in my recovery."[40]

While decriminalizing drugs has lofty goals, the reality is that it does not work. People need the real threat of criminal charges as a strong deterrent to drug use, which leads to addiction and crime. The experience of San Francisco highlights how decriminalizing drugs does not work to reduce drug use and addiction. In San Francisco public drug use is common, with drug users sprawled at transit stations and openly injecting drugs as people walk past. Beau Brady, a San Francisco resident and former heroin user, says that he gets asked several times a day to buy drugs near his apartment in the city's Tenderloin neighborhood. Brady says there has been a significant uptick in open drug use in the city, and he believes it is because drug users know there is little threat from the police. "They're doing it more blatantly now," he says. "They know they're not going to get in trouble or get arrested."[41]

"Most people struggling with addiction can't stop using drugs on their own. If they could, they wouldn't be addicted. However, many people in long-term recovery credit the motivation of court diversion programs with 'saving my life' or 'rescuing me from myself.'"[39]

—Heather Jefferis, executive director of the Oregon Council for Behavioral Health, and Se-ah-dom Edmo, cochair of the advocacy group Oregon Recovers

Source Notes

Overview: What Is Addiction?

1. Quoted in Allie Kirkman, "'Recovery Is Possible': Monticello Couple Share Stories of Beating Drug Addiction to Spread Hope," *Lafayette (IN) Journal & Courier*, November 29, 2020. www.jconline.com.
2. Quoted in Kirkman, "'Recovery Is Possible.'"
3. Quoted in Kirkman, "'Recovery Is Possible.'"
4. Quoted in Substance Abuse and Mental Health Services Administration, "SAMHSA Releases 2020 National Survey on Drug Use and Health," October 26, 2021. www.samhsa.gov.
5. Jason Good, "Debate Highlights Lasting Stigma of Addiction," *Addiction* (blog), Narconon Colorado, September 30, 2020. www.narconon-colorado.org.

Chapter One: Is Addiction a Disease or a Choice?

6. Quoted in US Department of Health and Human Services, Office of the Surgeon General, *Facing Addiction in America: The Surgeon General's Report on Alcohol, Drugs, and Health*. Washington, DC: US Department of Health and Human Services, 2016, p. v.
7. Jillian E. Hardee, "Science Says: Addiction Is a Chronic Disease, Not a Moral Failing," *Brain Health* (blog), Michigan Medicine, May 19, 2017. https://healthblog.uofmhealth.org.
8. Quoted in Genomind, "3 Things Genetic Testing Can Tell Us About Addiction," April 15, 2020. www.genomind.com.
9. Quoted in Kerry Nenn, "Point/Counterpoint: Is Addiction a Disease or a Choice?," American Addiction Centers, December 30, 2020. https://rehabs.com.
10. Quoted in Mary Caffrey, "Treat Addiction like a Chronic Disease, ACP Recommends," AJMC, April 3, 2017. www.ajmc.com.
11. Quoted in Anne Fletcher, "How and Why Addiction Is Not a Disease: A Neuroscientist Challenges Traditional Views," American Addiction Centers, November 4, 2019. https://rehabs.com.
12. Quoted in Fletcher, "How and Why Addiction Is Not a Disease."
13. Quoted in Vertava Health, "Can Adverse Childhood Experiences Cause Addiction?," 2021. https://vertavahealth.com.
14. Adi Jaffe, "6 Ways Your Environment Is Influencing Your Addiction," *All About Addiction*, (blog), *Psychology Today*, August 13, 2018. www.psychologytoday.com.

15. Quoted in Angela Haupt, "8 Women Share What Made Them Finally Decide to Get Sober," *Women's Health*, February 6, 2018. www.womenshealthmag.com.
16. Quoted in Haupt, "8 Women Share What Made Them Finally Decide to Get Sober."
17. Quoted in Haupt, "8 Women Share What Made Them Finally Decide to Get Sober."

Chapter Two: Should Medication-Assisted Treatment Be Used to Treat Addiction?

18. Sarah Gad, "My Drug Overdose Saved My Life. Now I'm Saving Others," *Marie Claire*, March 15, 2019. www.marieclaire.com.
19. Gad, "My Drug Overdose Saved My Life."
20. Gad, "My Drug Overdose Saved My Life."
21. Quoted in National Institutes of Health, "Methadone and Buprenorphine Reduce Risk of Death After Opioid Overdose," June 19, 2018. www.nih.gov.
22. Quoted in Bethany Bump, "Study: Lifting Addiction Meds Rule Would Save N.Y. Lives, Costs," *Albany (NY) Times Union*, December 6, 2019. www.timesunion.com.
23. Quoted in Jonathan Walsh, "How Medication Assisted Treatment Changed One Addict's Life," News 5 Cleveland, August 31, 2021. www.news5cleveland.com.
24. Quoted in Walsh, "How Medication Assisted Treatment Changed One Addict's Life."
25. Quoted in Northpoint Recovery, "Debate over Two Paths to Addiction Recovery Overshadows a Third Option," *Seattle Times*, October 30, 2019. www.seattletimes.com.
26. Quoted in Northpoint Recovery, "Debate over Two Paths to Addiction Recovery Overshadows a Third Option."
27. Quoted in Abby Goodnough, "In Rehab, 'Two Warring Factions': Abstinence vs. Medication," *New York Times*, December 29, 2018. www.nytimes.com.
28. Quoted in Goodnough, "In Rehab, 'Two Warring Factions.'"

Chapter Three: Should the United States Decriminalize Drugs?

29. John French, "Oregon Opportunity: Remove Criminal Penalties for Low-Level Possession of Controlled Substances," *Salem (OR) Statesman Journal*, September 18, 2020. www.statesmanjournal.com.

30. Quoted in Jan Hoffman, "She Went to Jail for a Drug Relapse. Tough Love or Too Harsh?," *New York Times*, June 4, 2018. www.nytimes.com.

31. Robert A. Lowe and Ray G. Stangeland, "Opinion: A 'Yes' on Measure 110 Will Ensure Oregon Treats Addiction as the Health Care Issue It Is," *The Oregonian* (Portland, OR), September 20, 2020. www.oregonlive.com.

32. John Hudak, "Marijuana's Racist History Shows the Need for Comprehensive Drug Reform," *How We Rise* (blog), Brookings Institution, June 23, 2020. www.brookings.edu.

33. Jag Davies, "4 Reasons Why the U.S. Needs to Decriminalize Drugs—and Why We're Closer than You Think," Drug Policy Alliance, July 9, 2017. https://drugpolicy.org.

34. Quoted in Naina Bajekal, "Want to Win the War on Drugs? Portugal Might Have the Answer," *Time*, August 1, 2018. https://time.com.

35. Quoted in Dirk Vanderhart, "Oregon's Pioneering Drug Law Raises More Questions than Answers in Early Months," OPB, October 27, 2021. www.opb.org.

36. Quoted in Vanderhart, "Oregon's Pioneering Drug Law Raises More Questions than Answers in Early Months."

37. John Sloca, "Our View: Decriminalizing Drugs Is Not the Answer," *Kenosha (WI) News*, February 20, 2020. www.kenoshanews.com.

38. *Seattle Times*, "Seattle's Persistent Crime Problem Demands Change," editorial, April 19, 2019. www.seattletimes.com.

39. Heather Jefferis and Se-ah-dom Edmo, "Opinion: Measure 110 Will Take Away Addiction Treatment and Is Bad for Kids," *The Oregonian* (Portland, OR), October 14, 2020. www.oregonlive.com.

40. Quoted in Maunette Loeks, "Women Share Stories of Recovery During Drug Court Celebration," *Scottsbluff (NE) Star Herald*, May 13, 2021. https://starherald.com.

41. Quoted in Jim Dalrymple and Black Montgomery, "Open Drug Use Has Exploded in San Francisco, Pushing the City's Liberal Image to the Limit," BuzzFeed News, May 9, 2018. www.buzzfeednew.com.

Addiction Facts

Substance Use

- Among Americans aged twelve years and older, 31.9 million are current illegal drug users (used within the past thirty days), according to the National Center for Drug Abuse Statistics (NCDAS).
- If alcohol and tobacco are included, 165 million, or 60.2 percent, of Americans aged twelve years or older currently abuse drugs, according to the NCDAS.
- More people aged eighteen to twenty-five use drugs (39 percent) compared to people aged twenty-six to twenty-nine (34 percent), according to the NCDAS.

Substance Use Disorders

- In 2020, 40.3 million people aged twelve or older (or 14.5 percent) had a substance use disorder in the past year, according to SAMHSA.
- The most common substance use disorders involve marijuana and prescription pain relievers.
- Drug use and substance use disorders are more likely to affect young males.
- According to the 2019 National Survey on Drug Use and Health, 9.5 million, or 3.8 percent, of adults over age eighteen have both a substance use disorder and a mental illness.
- More than half of people in state prisons and two-thirds of people awaiting sentencing in jail show signs of substance use disorder.

Addiction Treatment

- In 2020, 14.9 percent of people aged twelve or older needed substance use treatment in the past year, according to SAMHSA.
- Only one in ten people who need addiction treatment receive it.
- Among the 15 million individuals with alcohol use disorder, less than 8 percent receive treatment, according to the NCDAS.
- The stigma of addiction makes it more difficult to receive quality, compassionate treatment.

The Costs of Addiction

- Accidental drug overdose is a leading cause of death among persons under age forty-five, according to the NCDAS.
- Persons previously abusing drugs and recently released from prison are at the highest risk for overdose since their tolerance to the drug dropped while they were incarcerated.
- High-risk behaviors and drug abuse also result in much higher chances of contracting viral infections such as hepatitis or HIV.
- In 2017 the cost of drug abuse in the United States was nearly $272 billion, a number that includes costs related to crime, health care needs, lost work productivity, and other impacts on society, according to the NCDAS.

Related Organizations and Websites

American Addiction Centers

www.americanaddictioncenters.org

The American Addiction Centers is the country's leading provider of addiction treatment nationwide. Its website includes addiction and treatment information and other resources.

American Society for Addiction Medicine

www.asam.org

Founded in 1954, the American Society for Addiction Medicine is a professional medical society representing over six thousand physicians, clinicians, and associated professionals in the field of addiction medicine.

Brookings Institution

www.brookings.edu

The Brookings Institution is a nonprofit public policy organization based in Washington, DC. It strives to conduct in-depth research on problems facing society at the local, national, and global level, including addiction.

Cato Institute

www.cato.org

The Cato Institute is a public policy research organization that researches and promotes libertarian ideas in policy debates. Its website features information on a variety of issues, including addiction.

Centers for Disease Control and Prevention (CDC)

www.cdc.gov

The CDC is the premier public health agency in the United States. Its website includes the latest information about addiction, substance use disorders, and drug overdose.

National Harm Reduction Coalition
https://harmreduction.org
The National Harm Reduction Coalition is an advocacy organization that works to promote the well-being of people affected by drug use. It advances harm reduction strategies to decrease the harms of drug use. The coalition's website includes information about harm reduction strategies and how to get involved.

National Institute on Drug Abuse (NIDA)
www.drugabuse.gov
The NIDA is the leading federal agency supporting scientific research on drug use and its consequences. Its website provides information about drugs, research highlights, and recent news.

Pew Research Center
www.pewresearch.org
The Pew Research Center is a nonpartisan American think tank that provides information on social issues, public opinion, and demographic trends shaping the United States and the world, including substance use and addiction.

Substance Abuse and Mental Health Services Administration (SAMHSA) National Helpline
www.samhsa.gov/find-help/national-helpline
1 (800) 662-4357
SAMHSA is an agency in the US Department of Health and Human Services that works to reduce the impact of substance abuse and mental illness in America. It operates an around-the-clock help line for people facing mental or substance use disorders.

US Food and Drug Administration (FDA)
www.fda.gov
The FDA is a federal agency in the US Department of Health and Human Services. It is responsible for protecting public health by ensuring the safety of the US food supply, drugs, and other products.

For Further Research

Books

Sheri Mabry Bestor, *Substance Abuse*. Lanham, MD: Rowman & Little-field, 2021.

James J. Crist, *What's the Big Deal About Addictions? Answers and Help for Teens*. Minneapolis, MN: Free Spirit, 2021.

Nicole Horning, *Drug Addiction and Substance Use Disorders*. New York: Lucent, 2019.

Stephanie Lundquist-Arora, *Addiction: A Problem of Epidemic Proportions*. San Diego, CA: ReferencePoint, 2020.

David Sheff and Nic Sheff, *High: Everything You Want to Know About Drugs, Alcohol, and Addiction*. New York: Clarion, 2019.

Internet Sources

Addiction Center, "What Is Addiction?," 2021. www.addictioncenter.com.

American Psychiatric Association, "What Is a Substance Use Disorder?," 2020. www.psychiatry.org.

American Psychological Association, "Addictions," 2021. www.apa.org.

Drug Policy Alliance, "Drug Decriminalization," 2021. https://drugpolicy .org.

Adam Felman, "What Is Addiction?," Medical News Today, June 3, 2021. www.medicalnewstoday.com.

Wendy Sawyer and Peter Wagner, "Mass Incarceration: The Whole Pie 2020," Prison Policy Initiative, March 24, 2020. www.prisonpolicy.org.

Smart Recovery, "What Is Medication Assisted Treatment (MAT)?," October 2, 2018. www.smartrecovery.org.

Eric Westervelt, "Oregon's Pioneering Drug Decriminalization Experiment Is Now Facing the Hard Test," NPR, June 18, 2021. www.npr.org.

Index

Note: Boldface page numbers
indicate illustrations.

acamprosate, 29
addiction
  body's immune system and,
    32
  causes of, 8–10
  is choice
    absence of data for brain
      disease assertion, 21
    basic facts about, 13
    becomes habit, 22
    repetition of use supports
      pattern of thinking and
      feeling, 22
    role of environment and social
      factors, 23–24
    stopping is choice, 25
  is disease
    basic facts about, 13
    of brain, 14, 15–17, 22
    chronic, 20
    creation of physical
      dependency, 17–18
    genetic component, 10,
      18–20
    medical societies'
      classification, 15, 20
  medical personnel opinion of,
    as disease or choice, **23**
  risk of, 10–11
  types of, 7–8
  See also substance use
    disorder
adverse childhood events and
  addiction, 24

alcohol and dopamine release, 9
Alcoholics Anonymous, 34
American College of Physicians,
  20
American Medical Association,
  15
American Society of Addiction
  Medicine, 15, 48–49
Associated Press-NORC Center
  for Public Affairs Research
  survey, 16

behavioral addiction, basic facts
  about, 8
Benson, Carly, 24–25
Blacks and drug possession
  arrests, 43
Brady, Beau, 51
Brady, Kathleen, 19
brain
  addiction is disease of, 14
  areas involved in, 16
  changes in brain chemistry
    and function, 15–17
  development of new
    pathways and pruning of
    old, 22
  dopamine releases by, 9, 17
  retention of memories of
    pleasure of dopamine, 17
buprenorphine
  approved as MAT medication,
    29
  can be abused, 36
  is opioid, 34
  reduces chance of death from
    opioid overdose, 31

Centers for Disease Control and Prevention, 32, 42
criminal records, consequences of having, 43

Davies, Jag, 45
deaths
    increase in, from drug overdoses, 42
    MATs decrease, 30–31
    from methadone overdoses, 36
decriminalization of drugs
    meaning of, 40–41
    in Oregon, 42
    US should adopt
        basic facts about, 39
        consequences of arrests hurt families, 43–44
        ending punishment approach to drug use, 40–41
        has been successful in other countries, 45
        medical practitioner support, 42
        public health and safety will benefit, 41–42
        racial and ethnic disparities in enforcement of drug possession laws, 43
        resources could be directed to improve treatment, **44**
    US should not adopt
        basic facts about, 39
        crimes committed to buy drugs, 48
        criminal justice system provides an important path to treatment, **49**, 50–51
        decriminalization has not been successful in US, 47–48, 51

threat of criminal charges is tool to deter people from using illegal drugs, 46–48
deportations, 44
detox, traditional, 27
diabetes, 14–15
Diagnostic and Statistical Manual of Mental Disorders, 8
disease(s)
    basic facts about, 14–15
    causes of, 23
    drug-injection equipment and spread of, 32
    identical twins and, 19–20
    MAT reduces infectious, 32
disulfiram, 29
domestic abuse, 48–49
dopamine, 9, 17
Drabiak, Katherine, 33
drug addiction
    basic facts about, 7–8
    prescribed painkillers and, 6, **9**
Drug Policy Alliance, 43
drugs
    daily number of incarcerations for, 43
    dopamine release and, 9
    type of, and addiction risk and, 10
    way used and addiction risk, 10–11
    withdrawal symptoms and type of, 18

Eldred, Julie, 41–42
environmental risk factors, 10, 19, 23–24
epigenetics, 10, 19
ethnicity and drug possession arrests and, 43

family history of addiction, 10, 19

Fonseca, Gonçalo, 45
French, John, 40, 41

Gad, Sarah, 29
gambling addiction, 8
genetics, 10, 18–20
Good, Jason, 12
Grifell, Marc, 21

habits, described, 22
Hardee, Jillian E., 17
heart disease, 14, 18
Henry, Dock, 6–7
Hudak, John, 43–44

identical twins, 19–20
incarceration, daily number of, for
    drugs, 43

Jaffe, Adi, 24
Jefferis, Heather, 50
*Journal of Substance Abuse
    Treatment*, 48
*Journal of the American Medical
    Association*, 31

LaBelle, Regina, 7
Labuda, Dan, 34
Latinos and drug possession
    arrests, 43
Lewis, Marc, 22
Lowe, Robert A., 42

MacMaster, Sam, 35
medication-assisted treatment
    (MAT)
    basic facts about, 11, 26,
        28–29
    medications approved by FDA
        for, 29
    should be used
        effectiveness of, **28**

reduces infectious disease,
    32
results in early stabilization
    and ability to increase
    coping skills, 28
saves lives, 30–31
saves money, 31
success rate as proof, **28**
should not be used
    is substituting one opioid for
        another, 34–35
    methadone and
        buprenorphine can be
        abused, 36
    possible side effects, 36–38,
        37
    results in polysubstance
        abuse, 33
methadone
    approved as MAT medication,
        29
    can be abused, 36
    is opioid, 34
    possible effects of use of,
        37–38
    reduces chance of death from
        opioid overdose, 31
Morse, Eric, 27
Murthy, Vivek, 15

naltrexone, 29
National Institute on Drug Abuse,
    10, 36
National Institutes of Health, 30
National Survey on Drug Use
    and Health (2020, SAMHSA),
    21
neurotransmitters, 9, 17
Newbold, Donna, 19–20
Newman-Polk, Lisa, 42

O'Neill, Maeve, 24

opioids
  MAT medications are, 34–35
  MAT medications decrease
    frequency of use of, 33
  MATs decrease deaths of users
    of, 30–31
  weaken body's immune system,
    32
Oregon, 42, 47

peer pressure, 24–25
Portugal, 45
Price, Tom, 34
Prison Policy Initiative, 43, **44**
prisons, availability of drugs in,
  41
public opinion
  in America on addiction as
    disease of choice, **16**
  of medical personnel on
    addiction as disease of
    choice, **23**

race and drug possession
  arrests, 43
Ramsey, Heather, 34–35
rehabilitation programs (rehab),
  traditional, 27
relapses, 17, 27
Richardson, Reginald, Sr., 46, 47
risks factors of addiction, 10–11

Samuels, Paul, 31
San Francisco, 51
Schedule II controlled
  substances, 36
Schreiber, MacKenzie, 50–51
Seattle, Washington, 49–50
Seattle Times, 49–50
Sloca, John, 48

social pressures, 24–25
Stangeland, Ray G., 42
Substance Abuse and Mental
  Health Services Administration
  (SAMHSA)
  effects of adverse childhood
    events, 24
  number of Americans with
    substance use disorder, 7, 21
substance use disorder
  number of Americans with, 7,
    21
  violent behaviors and, 48–49

Thomas, Megan, 31
treatment
  abstinence-based, 33–34
  basic facts about, 11
  criminal justice system provides
    an important path to, **49**,
    50–51
  effectiveness of different types
    of, **28**
  traditional, 27
  See also medication-assisted
    treatment (MAT)
twins, 19–20

US Food and Drug Administration
  (FDA), 28–29

Vezina, Tony, 48
Volkow, Nora D., 14, 30

withdrawal symptoms
  described, 18, 35
  MAT medications prevent, 29
  physical dependency and,
    17–18
World Health Organization, 32

Picture Credits

Cover: iordani/Shutterstock.com

 9: Steve Heap/Shutterstock.com
16: Maury Aaseng
23: Maury Aaseng
28: Maury Aaseng
37: Maury Aaseng
44: Maury Aaseng
49: Maury Aaseng

About the Author

Carla Mooney is the author of many books for young adults and children. She lives in Pittsburgh, Pennsylvania, with her husband and three children.